What's going on out there?

Understanding today's world

John Benton

EVANGELICAL PRESS
Faverdale North Industrial Estate, Darlington, DL3 0PH, England

Evangelical Press USA
P. O. Box 825, Webster, New York 14580, USA

e-mail: sales@evangelicalpress.org

web: http://www.evangelicalpress.org

© Evangelical Press 2003. All rights reserved. No part of this publication may be reproduced, stored in a retrieval system or transmitted, in any form, or by any means, electronic, mechanical, photocopying, recording or otherwise, without the prior permission of the publishers.

First published October 2003
Second impression July 2004

British Library Cataloguing in Publication Data available

ISBN 0 85234 555 0

Scripture quotations in this publication are from the Holy Bible, New International Version. Copyright © 1973, 1978, 1984, International Bible Society. Used by permission of Hodder & Stoughton, a member of the Hodder Headline Group. All rights reserved.

Printed and bound in Great Britain by Aztec Colour Print, Washington, Tyne & Wear.

What's going on out there?

It was winter. Our neighbour was returning from a day's work. As she walked up the road she was startled to see all the lights on in her house and the silhouettes of large men moving around inside. 'What on earth is going on?' she thought in alarm. She rushed to her front door, anxious and angry.

It turned out to be a drugs raid. The police had arrested her son and were searching the house for illegal substances. The pressures on single parents are heavy, and all unbeknown to her, her boy had begun to experiment with drugs.

She was due to come round for a meal with us that evening, but understandably she dropped in to call it off. How did she feel about her son? She felt both sorry for and angry with him at the same time. As a mother her heart went out to him, understanding the difficulties and disappointments in his life, which had led him to take comfort in drugs. But at the same time she was very angry. She said she 'could have killed him' for getting himself into this and exposing her and the rest of the family to all the ramifications of the situation. It is possible to feel genuine love and real anger at the same time — and for the same person.

That is how it is with God and the world. The Bible tells us that he loves us deeply, yet alongside this, it speaks of God's rightful anger against what it calls sin. Sin is failing to meet God's standards and breaking his laws.

Love and anger are expressed at the same time. 'How can that happen?' we might wonder. Yet as the story of our neighbour makes clear, we can feel love and anger simultaneously. It is a fallacy to think that justifiable anger excludes love, or love excludes the possibility of anger.

This truth of the dual love and anger of God is not a pleasant one. However, it is the key to understanding what is happening in our society. As we look out on today's world, people are concerned and confused about what they see. For many, it is becoming a more prosperous world, but at the same time more violent. In the West we are more educated than ever, and our technology is amazingly advanced, yet simultaneously, family, community and neighbourliness seem to be breaking down. As the numbers attending church decline, crime levels rise — the prison population in Britain has recently reached an all-time high. The Bible spells out that this is not a coincidence: if we turn from God and his blueprint for a healthy society, it is not surprising that our social order begins to fragment.

If God has a blueprint and plan for humanity to be healthy, it is worth looking at it, not only to understand what has gone wrong, but also to discover if

What's going on out there?

there is a solution. God's blueprint, or framework, is revealed to us in the Bible. As we dig into this powerful resource, we discover some uncomfortable things about ourselves, and yet, we can also find a way by which our lives can be helped and guided. But most importantly, we will discover how we can be forgiven by God and receive what the Bible calls 'eternal life' — that is, a new quality of life now, that extends past death and lasts for ever and ever.

God's wrath now?

When we think of God's anger, generally we think of earthquakes, apocalyptic disasters and thunderbolts from heaven. Many a cynic paints a picture of the ancient biblical cities of sin, Sodom and Gomorrah, being destroyed by fire from above, only to sneer at the possibility of such judgements ever happening. And as we survey our godless Western society, there is a distinct lack of fire from heaven. So how does the anger and judgement of God show itself today?

One strand of the Bible's teaching equates God's judgement with the reversal, or unravelling, of the good world he originally created. It is through the undoing, or unmaking, of that which God made 'very good' at the beginning of the world, that he expresses his condemnation. Let me give a couple of examples of this.

God created the first man, Adam, out of the ground. Precisely how he did that is not at issue here. But Genesis, the first book in the Bible, tells us, 'The LORD

God formed the man from the dust of the ground and breathed into his nostrils the breath of life, and the man became a living being.'[a] The Bible's narrative goes on to tell us how, after the initial perfect creation, a great tragedy occurred, when this first man, Adam, rebelled against the loving God and fell into sin. The judgement of God came upon Adam for what he had done; there was a sentence, or punishment: Adam would die. God pronounced that Adam would return to the ground, 'for dust you are and to dust you will return'.[b] The judgement was that, in a sense, Adam was to be unmade: creation was reversed.

The consequence of Adam's action is that all humankind is willingly trapped in sin. The rebellion of Adam was sown into his genes, as it were; and this expressed itself more and more as the ensuing generations came into being. The growing human population became increasingly wicked, until God judged the world in the great flood. The fossil record found in the earth's geological layers is evidence of the reality of that gigantic destruction. The water that Genesis tells us covered the world at the very beginning, once more submerged everything. God's creation of the dry land was temporarily reversed. Once again, his judgement can be seen as an undoing of creation.

There are other ways in which this theme of good being unravelled surfaces throughout the Bible. Understanding God's right and just anger as the reversal, or unravelling, of creation throws an important light on what is happening today. It helps us to understand what the Bible means when it says, 'The wrath [or anger] of God is being revealed from heaven against all the godlessness and wickedness of men who suppress the truth by their wickedness.'[c] Much of what is going on in our society today is not only human wickedness, but is actually an outworking of God's judgement upon us.

This concurrence of human sin and God's judgement seems strange, but on further reflection makes sense. It is a common experience with most products we buy that if we ignore the maker's instructions we run into trouble. If we do not read the recommended oven temperature on the pizza box, our meal will be reduced to a blackened, inedible mess. If we put diesel into a car made for unleaded fuel it will soon shudder to a halt. Similarly when we ignore God, our Maker, and his instructions we run into trouble. As people reject God and his laws, pursuing their own agendas, they bring difficulty, darkness and despair upon themselves and their communities.

The Bible tells us that we are experiencing a kind of judgement in slow-motion. The anger, or wrath, of God is 'being revealed'. It is not a simple, instantaneous event — it is an ongoing process, unfolding more and more of God's displeasure. The fireball from heaven is shattering, spectacular and immediate, but God has other, slower ways of showing his anger that are equally devastating. A seaside house built on the top of a chalk cliff does not have to be destroyed by lightning from the sky. The steady pounding of the waves eroding the coastline beneath will just as surely undermine the cliffs and bring them and the house crashing into the sea.

Unravelling the world

There are many precious things on which peace, well-being and liberty in a nation depend, but which are gradually being eroded, or have been lost already, to our society over recent years.

Let me list a few of them:

- the uniqueness of human beings as made in the image of God

- the sanctity of human life
- the unity and equality of the races as descended from one ancestral human pair
- the general consensus on the difference between right and wrong
- the personal responsibility and accountability of the individual for their actions
- the blessing of a weekly day of rest from work for the community
- the distinctive difference between male and female as positive for both sexes
- the loving traditional family as the basic unit of society
- the caring government of the earth and its resources
- the right to a home and to be active in gainful employment.

The early chapters of the Bible tell us that such things were part of God's 'very good' creation; they were built into the world for humanity's benefit and for his glory.[d] But if that is true, then much of what passes for 'progress' and 'liberation' in the modern world is actually an unravelling of this 'goodness', and a slow but sure outworking of God's judgement.

Take, for example, the matter of personal responsibility. Increasingly, society is moving away from this cornerstone on which the rule of law is built. We are descending ever more relentlessly into an outlook that precludes individuals from being looked upon as accountable for their actions. But how can such a society be governed? Psychological theories may have some validity, but once they dominate the cultural landscape in such a way as to explain *all* human actions in terms of upbringing, brain chemistry and social pressures, then the idea of personal responsibility becomes a nonsense.

Even humanists, who extol humanity without any reference to God, are worried: 'There are no longer sinners,' wrote Frank Furedi in *The Spectator* recently, 'only addictive personalities.' He went on to comment on the traditional list of the seven deadly sins, and said that they have been transformed into behavioural problems that require treatment, not castigation. For example, take lust: those who might once have been denounced as lustful are now said to be 'addicted' to sex and in need of therapy. Gluttons, likewise, are suffering from an eating disorder. Uncontrolled anger now takes forms such as 'road rage' and calls for stress management techniques. Greed and envy have become a form of 'shopaholism'. Even some forms of sloth have been medicalized. As for the last of the seven deadly sins, pride, this has actually been turned into a virtue: almost all problems today are blamed on lack of self-esteem. Furedi concludes, 'I'm not keen on the idea of sin. But given the choice of being powerless in the face of God, or an impotent client of a therapist, I side with the Church.'[1]

This is more than a jovial piece of tongue-in-cheek social comment. With such a philosophy of non-responsibility, it seems ever more difficult for our judicial system to uphold law and order. Clever defence lawyers cannot only find loopholes in the law, but also excuses for crime. Thus the police find it increasingly difficult to secure convictions. Surely only disaster awaits a community in which no one is responsible for anything.

Take another example. We are in the process of throwing away the idea of lifelong marriage. Half a century ago, divorce was rare and cohabiting even rarer. But there has been an immense rise in the popularity of merely living together instead of getting married. In 1979, 11% of all non-married women between 18 and 49 years were cohabiting. In 1998-99 this had more than doubled to 29%. The lifestyle data from the 2001 census in Britain showed that the number of households headed by married couples has fallen below 50% for the first time. The statistics tell us that cohabiting relationships involving children are far less stable than marriages.² Half of all cohabiting parents part within ten years, compared to one in eight married parents. Once separation has taken place, only 45% of children of cohabiting couples remain in contact with both parents. This causes all kinds of misery, insecurity and instability for many children. Very often divorced fathers, who have started a new relationship, are not able to support two families, and so poverty enters the equation too. All this leads to the multitude of rootless, insecure youngsters that we see in our society — and we wonder why we have problems with teenage crime. Again, we see that good is being unravelled.

The Bible mentions sexual impurity, followed by homosexuality and lesbianism, as prime examples of departures from God's creation pattern in the sexual area of life.ᵉ God is not a killjoy. He made us to be sexual beings, and to enjoy the gift of sexual relations within male-female marriage. But departure from God's pattern in this area causes all kinds of problems. Whether it is among heterosexuals, homosexuals or bisexuals, sexual promiscuity has been a major contributor to the tragedy of the AIDS epidemic that now threatens the lives of so many people. Similarly, despite government efforts to promote so-called 'safe sex', medical professionals continue to be alarmed at the numbers of teenage pregnancies and the spread of sexually transmitted diseases.³

This is not scare-mongering. These are just a few instances that illustrate the way in which the good that God built into the world is being unravelled: the wrath of God is being revealed.

The Bible does not teach a neat one-to-one correspondence between suffering in our lives in this world and personal sin. Certainly, for example, the trauma and pain experienced by children when their family breaks up is rarely, if ever, their fault. But our society as a whole is caught up under the judgement of God, and this impinges even on innocent individual lives, both directly and indirectly. According to the Bible, Adam's sin cast a shadow over the whole world, and as we pursue his rejection of God we find ourselves in ever-increasing difficulties.

Suppressing the truth

This might seem strange but God originally intended pain as a good gift. The body's network of nerve ends, which relay signals to the brain so that we experience pain, is an alarm system to cause us to avoid whatever is threatening or attacking us. When we put our hand accidentally on to a hot stove we feel the pain and quickly withdraw it, and are saved further damage. We pity the people who have lost sensitivity, and burn themselves without even realizing what is happening. And what the nervous system does to protect us bodily, our consciences were meant to do to protect us morally and spiritually. Therefore, we would expect that when it becomes clear to us that certain actions and lifestyles are bringing pain upon individuals, and trouble upon society as a whole, we would take note of the warning signals and change our ways.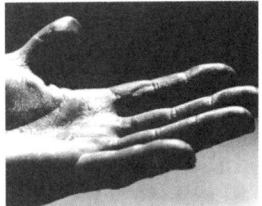

But surprisingly that is not what happens. Rather, pursuing our rebellion against God, initiated by the first human, Adam, we either ignore the problems, or try to explain them away. Remember the Bible's words, 'The wrath of God is being revealed from heaven against all the godlessness and wickedness of men who *suppress the truth* by their wickedness.'[f] The truth we do not wish to face is stamped on and driven underground, so that we can pursue our own agendas unhindered.

A few years ago the most disturbing evidence came to light concerning the risks to health, which threatens those who engage in homosexual practice. The authors of the research analysed 6,500 obituaries from the American gay press and compared them with obituaries from conventional newspapers. Whereas the average age of death for straight married men was seventy-five years, the average age for homosexual deaths was much much lower.⁴ Such facts do not make the headlines and they do not appear in school materials concerning sex education. Whether deliberately or by sheer neglect, the truth is suppressed. Again, from my own experience, school teachers have said that the children who have behavioural problems, poor concentration and the consequent low attainment are often children growing up in broken homes.

But such instances of the concealment of truth are actually mere symptoms that flow from a far deeper suppression of the truth: they are the inevitable consequences of denying God. The reason we do not like to face the fact that immorality and lawlessness bring trouble is that we want to chase after the impossible dream that we can live life any way we choose. Ultimately that attitude goes right back to wanting to live without accountability to God.

The Bible tells us that people do 'not think it worth while to retain the knowledge of God'.ᵍ Following the footsteps of Adam, our common ancestor, our rebellious hearts do not wish to be subject to our Creator. We do not want God telling us what to do. Therefore, we convince ourselves that God does not exist.

The world is not whatever we have the skill and resolve to make it. This is God's world, and the greatest suppression of the truth, the most insidious self-deception from which all other lies about human beings and what is good for them flow, is the pretence that the Creator is not there.

The Bible tells us that 'what may be known about God is plain ... because God has made it plain...'ʰ It goes on to explain that, all around us, creation is an all-embracing witness to the fact of God. People are without excuse in denying God because, 'Since the creation of the world God's invisible qualities — his eternal power and divine nature — have been clearly seen, being understood from what has been made, so that men are without excuse.'ⁱ

What's going on out there?

Piecing together the jigsaw

Popular 'sound-bite' science peddles the concept of the world coming about through chance. It gives the impression that, given enough time, random collisions between fundamental particles could create all the order and beauty we see on planet earth.

Imagine taking a 500-piece jigsaw puzzle, separating all the pieces and mixing them up in the box. Then a good space is cleared on the living room carpet. With the lid off the box, now you throw all the jigsaw pieces up into the air and see what happens. How will all the pieces land? What is the chance of perhaps two or three pieces joining up correctly? It is very unlikely.

But go on from there and ask the greater question. What is the chance of all the pieces somehow falling so that they join up appropriately to make the picture? Would it ever happen? If you repeated the experiment 100 times, or even 1000 times, would the jigsaw ever fall together? We all know that even if we spent every moment of our lives collecting up the jigsaw pieces and throwing them again, the puzzle would never assemble itself by this purely random process. Even though all the pieces are specifically made to fit together, it would never assemble itself.

Our world is far more complicated than a 500-piece jigsaw. The idea that our world assembled itself out of pure chance is unrealistic. To insist that there is no God is to suppress the truth.

The human body itself is far more complex than a jigsaw puzzle. For example, the fact that our blood coagulates when we cut ourselves is vital to our survival. Yet coagulation involves at least ten separate factors which are triggered by the enzymic action of the previous link in the chain. If just one of those links was missing we might either bleed to death or all our blood coagulate. Could such a mechanism have come about by chance? And yet the human body is just one piece of the gigantic picture that makes the earth we inhabit. And the earth is just one piece in the astonishing jigsaw puzzle of the universe. To insist our origins are the product of blind chance is astounding self-deception.

Actually, in a sense, the jigsaw analogy does not go far enough. Though it makes nonsense of the 'chance world' scenario, it in fact paints a far too optimistic picture of that possibility. To make a true parallel between the jigsaw experiment and the world coming about by chance you would have to explain not only how the jigsaw pieces could come together randomly, but also where the pieces of the jigsaw came from in the first place. When we considered the jigsaw analogy we accepted that the jigsaw pieces had already been manufactured. But for the world to come about by chance you must start with absolutely nothing, or else you will be left asking where your original material came from, and therefore have no ultimate explanation. You must start with no time, no materials, and no scientific laws with which to work. Science does a tremendous job of exploring and harnessing our physical world, and we rejoice in the many benefits of technological advance, yet for science to be hijacked into trying to give an ultimate explanation of everything from nothing is beyond its capabilities. To deny the Creator is a further suppression of the truth.

God gave them over

This suppression of truth brings about a second strand to understanding the anger of God. Because we do not wish to retain any knowledge of God, the Bible tells us that God lets us go our own way. He lets us believe what we want to believe. He lets us go after what we want to go after. In a way, he gives us what we want — or to use the Bible's own language, 'God gave them over' to sinful desires, shameful lusts and a depraved mind.[j]

Yet, even though people are in rebellion against God, in his love, he still upholds our existence and enables us to live out our lives. When people pursue their selfishness, they can only do so because of God's kindness to them. The angry atheist can only shake his fist against God because God empowers him to do so. The sinner can only sin because he or she chooses to misuse the moments in time God has granted for life. God lets us go our own way, but he still sustains us. This goodness of God ought to lead us to take stock and understand that his love deserves a better response from us. It ought to lead us to turn back to him, but sadly it does not.

When God allows people to go their own way, it is their desires and lusts that come to the fore. Not wanting to retain the knowledge of God, having suppressed the truth, the world no longer makes much sense. Philosophy breaks down. People's thinking becomes twisted. They find that their minds are not a satisfactory guide to life, so they turn to their emotions instead. 'Feel good' begins to rule, and because the sexual drive is bound up with some of the most intense and pleasurable feelings that human beings can experience, society becomes enslaved to lusts of various kinds.

We have become a society captivated by sensualism. Our cinema, our TV soap operas, our glossy magazines and our tabloid newspapers have succumbed to domination by sexual innuendo and provocative images. It is sad to observe that the Internet, with all its vast possibilities for good, is so extensively used to advertise and access pornography.

The Bible brings interesting light to bear on this: it says that people 'are darkened in their understanding and separated from the life of God because of the ignorance that is in them due to the hardening of their hearts. Having lost all sensitivity, they have given themselves over to sensuality so as to indulge in every kind of impurity, with a continual lust for more.'[k] At this point the Bible speaks of people having 'given themselves over' to lust, whereas in the passage quoted earlier, it speaks of 'God giving them over'. Here is a terrible concurrence. When people give themselves over to such things it is a sign that God has given them over. This is a second aspect of the present manifestation of the wrath of God.

Man, materialism and magic

Interestingly, the Bible gives us another way of explaining the present situation from a slightly different angle: the right use of our senses. Originally, God made us in his image to worship him. We are therefore creatures who love to be amazed and excited, and who can give praise to that which causes us wonder. Our five senses were given to us, partly, to drink in all the great experiences and sensations which God made legitimately possible for us in the world, so that then, out of gratitude, we might worship him.[5]

But having rejected God, people tend to worship creation, rather than the Creator.[l] Things take the place of God. We worship material things, living for our homes, or our holidays, or the next new car. We love the excitement of sport, and the sound of music, and the taste of great food. These experiences thrill our senses, but do not lead us to praise God. We love our meals, our money, our entertainment. We 'worship' sports heroes, comedians, film idols and rock stars instead of God. The cult of celebrity has become the new religion. We idolize people who, for all their true talent, are only human beings, like us. This is what we have chosen and God has given us over to such foolishness.

But, on top of this, people cannot live totally materialistic lives; deep down we know there is a spiritual dimension to our existence. So, having rejected God, our hearts yearn for something else, something transcendent: this spiritual dimension of our lives desires to be satisfied. Today, across Western society, people are returning to ancient pagan beliefs — indeed, bookshops in our high streets offer a wide and diverse range of ways of 'connecting' into some 'spiritual' domain: crystals, visualization, astrology, wicca, channelling, spiritism, altered states of consciousness, shamanism and meditations are but a few. Old and almost forgotten pagan beliefs are being revived in Neo-Paganism, and Eastern religions are deluging our society. Such things would have been thought madness a generation ago, but now they are becoming an accepted part of our culture — ours is a very 'New Age'. Although all of this is meant to give enlightenment, in reality it brings utter spiritual darkness, without any moral framework, or glimpse of God; participants become enmeshed, bound and lost.

The good that God built into the world is being eroded as we have turned away from him. God has given us over to a way of thinking that refuses to see the foolishness of the direction we are pursuing, even when it brings pain and damage to our lives. Why are we witnessing the disintegration of community and care and respect for the elderly? Why, though we are more educated and more prosperous than ever, are we a society in decay? Why has there been a doubling of alcohol-related deaths in the past two decades?[6]

The ultimate answer is that we are caught up in a society that is undergoing the judgement of God. It is a judgement in slow-motion, which is undermining the stability of the world. That is the Bible's understanding of our times — it is a very solemn and sobering thought.

Secularization

As a young man growing up in the 1960s, it was obvious to me that the times were changing. I became interested in the direction secular society was taking. Surprisingly, on consideration, this turned into an evidence for the truth of biblical faith. In the previous century many critics had scoffed at Christianity, proclaiming that the Christian faith was irrelevant and no longer required in a modern world. In particular, they had asserted that it is perfectly possible to have a secular society that is morally upright and decent. People like the great playwright George Bernard Shaw argued for this. We did not need the 'outdated doctrines' of Christ and the Bible. Human beings are reasonable, we were told, and would inevitably choose the good.[7]

In a sense, in the Western world, the twentieth century was the acid test of that theory. Starting gradually, but gathering its full momentum mid-century, the inexorable progress of secularization more or less ran its course in the last hundred years. Had secularization prevailed, and yet the country remained decent, it would have added weight to the argument that the Christian faith was irrelevant. If the nation had deserted the church and turned away from religion with crime statistics not rising, no eruption of divorce and pornography, increasingly efficient and sensitive care for the vulnerable, then that would have been evidence that the biblical view of things should be called into question. But of course, instead, our culture has slid into new depths of violence, immorality and selfishness. The history of the last century has only served to demonstrate the continuing degeneration of society, and has done nothing but confirm the biblical analysis of the world.

When people turn from God and become secularized, it inevitably follows that society falls into moral degeneracy. God gives us up to our own foolish and sinful desires. The evidence for this surrounds us all every day. We are inevitably driven to the conclusion that our Western world is undergoing the judgement of God.

What are we to conclude?

If this is the case, then there are conclusions that follow. There are three deductions that the Bible would encourage us to make, and it is to those we now turn.

It is popularly held that if God is there then he is totally benign. But the Bible tells us something very different, and the evidence of what is happening in our society confirms that. God is holy, and though he loves us, at the same time his chastisement is at work. We should not condemn God for his anger. After all, we ourselves are rightly angry at much of the crime and abuse which goes on in our day.

The justifiable wrath of God does not reveal a defect in God's character. Rather, love and anger go together — they are two sides of the same coin. Going back to the incident mentioned at the beginning of this booklet, it was because the mother loved her son who was on drugs that she was so angry with him. Her anger expressed her emotional involvement with him. God's anger is not irrational; it is not due to some divine irritability. The Bible emphasizes repeatedly the patience of God, but God's anger is rightly stirred by human sin; it is provoked by the fact that we ignore our Creator, we turn from what is good, suppress the truth and then delight in our foolish and sinful ways.

Judgement coming

The first deduction the Bible would encourage us to make from what we have considered concerning our present society is that if God's justifiable

indignation is active now, then we should take very seriously the idea of a judgement to come. Contemporary cynics mock the very thought of this. But this is no surprise, for Scripture even predicts that there would be 'scoffers' who would deride the idea of a coming judgement.[m] Yet, whatever the sneers to the contrary, the Bible tells us clearly there certainly will come a final eternal judgement for sin.

Death is not the end; one day we will all stand before God and have to give an account of the way we have lived our lives. The coming day will not be a day when society is judged, but when individuals are judged. The Bible explains: 'God "will give to each person according to what he has done". To those who by persistence in doing good seek glory, honour and immortality, he will give eternal life. But for those who are self-seeking and who reject the truth and follow evil, there will be wrath and anger. There will be trouble and distress for every human being who does evil ... but glory, honour and peace for everyone who does good.'[n]

This is eminently just and fair: people will get what they deserve. The great problem for us all is that if we are honest with ourselves, we know we have not lived well. We have not persistently and consistently practised good; we have chosen to live without reference to God our Creator; we have been self-seeking; we have told lies; we have 'worshipped' money and material things rather than God. In one way or another, we have gone along with our immoral culture. As the Bible says, 'All have sinned and fall short of the glory of God.'[o]

Unforgiven sinners receiving God's eternal judgement will be cast into hell, meaning that they will be cast out of the presence of God for ever. But God is the source and supply of all that is good. There is no good apart from him. Hell is therefore the place where all good is removed.

This does not happen because God is unfair, but because it is what we deserve. It is what we have chosen. We did not want God. We 'did not think it worth while to retain the knowledge of God'.[p] God's judgement is the final and unalterable confirmation for eternity of the choice we have made in time. It will not be a judgement in slow motion, it will be a once and for all condemnation that unleashes all the righteous fury of almighty God that sinners have stored up through unrepentant pursuit of a life without God.

How do we know that God judges sin? How do we know that this is not just some scare story put around by Christian preachers? The answer is because his judgement is already seen to be at work in our society, in our time. All we have to do is open our eyes. The fragmentation of communities, the break-down of family life and the moral downhill slide of the world we live in shows us that God's judgement is already at work. Our politicians recognize many of the problems, but no matter how sincere or skilful, they are not able to stop the slow landslide. Not long ago in Britain a certain prime minister called the country 'back to basics', only to have to quickly retract when it was felt he might be calling for a moral crusade. Politicians cannot stop the rot. It is the wrath of God — judgement is being worked out. And judgement now is the sure evidence and certain sign of judgement to come.

But if that were the only deduction we are meant to make from witnessing the slow-motion judgement of God in our society, then we would have missed the real point. Thankfully we can also see God's love in what is going on in our world.

Jesus Christ

The Bible tells us that this same God who is justifiably angry loves us deeply and desires us to be saved from the consequences of our rebellion and sin.

Just as certain as his displeasure is the evidence of his love.

What is being worked out in our society is indeed judgement; but, as we have seen, it is a judgement in slow-motion. It is not swift. It is protracted: it has been taking place over many years. The reason for this is that God is giving us time and opportunity to turn back to him. That is not to say that our society will never fall or be overthrown. Eventually, after years of erosion by the pounding waves of the sea, the cliff will fall. There may well come an end to the godless Western materialistic democracies. Who knows how long it might be until chaos comes, and the Western world becomes ungovernable?

But, as yet, that end has not arrived. God is still giving us time as individuals and as a society to turn to his Son, Jesus Christ, and be saved. Western society has never been perfect. But its strengths have historically been rooted in the Christian faith. The wheels of judgement at present grind slowly, because God's great heart still goes out to us that we might turn back and be saved.[q] Like the mother of that addicted son mentioned at the beginning, God is angry, but at the same time he is full of compassion and love, and still seeks our good. The Bible insists repeatedly that the Lord is 'the compassionate and gracious God, slow to anger, abounding in love'.[r]

How can this tension between God's wrath and his love be resolved? The remarkable proclamation of the Bible is that there are two places where sin is finally judged. One of these places is where unrepentant sinners suffer the consequences they have brought on themselves by their sin — the place called hell. But remarkably there is another place where sin is dealt with. That place is the cross of Jesus Christ, God's Son, where he paid the price for sin, once and for all, for everyone who trusts in him and turns back to God.

The death of Jesus Christ is the great expression of the love of God that enables sinners like us to be saved from judgement to come and given eternal life. This is the good news that the Bible reveals to us. It shows us that God's anger against sin is *being* revealed, but it also explains that, through Jesus Christ, the way of rescue *has been* revealed. It is our sin that damns us, but God provides a righteousness that saves us.

'But now a righteousness from God, apart from law, has been made known ... this righteousness from God comes through faith in Jesus Christ to all who believe. There is no difference, for all have sinned and fall short of the glory of God, and are justified freely by his grace through the redemption that came by Christ Jesus. God presented him as a sacrifice of atonement, through faith in his blood ... he did it to demonstrate his justice at the present time, so as to be just and the one who justifies the man who has faith in Jesus.'[8]

The word 'justified' is most often employed these days in connection with word processing on our computers. We use it to describe lining up the edge of the text on one, or both, sides of the paper. We put the text in a straight line. But here, in the Bible, 'justified' is about being in line in a different sense. The word 'justified' is actually a word from a court of law; and refers to the declaration of a judge at the end of a trial. When a judge declares a defendant guilty, that is called 'condemnation'. But when a judge pronounces the defendant not guilty, and acquitted, he is declaring that the defendant is innocent and in line with the law. That declaration of innocence is therefore called 'justification'.

The wonderful message of the Christian good news is that, although there is a great and fearful day of judgement coming, and although we have all broken God's law, yet nevertheless, because of what the Lord Jesus Christ did at the cross, everyone who believes in him is justified. God is giving away pardons for judgement day now. Believers in Christ are declared acquitted by God. Through faith in Christ we are no longer out of line with God and his law. We escape judgement and are accepted by God through putting our trust in his Son, Jesus Christ.

As we saw earlier, when the first man Adam rebelled against God it brought death. The Bible puts it like this: 'The wages of sin is death.'[t] But God sent his own Son, Jesus, into the world. Jesus never sinned. He lived a perfect life. Then at Calvary, he, the innocent one, died in the place of sinners. He has atoned for our sins, and appeased God's wrath, for all who trust in him. He died to pay our debt and rose again from the dead to demonstrate that the price for sin had been fully met. Jesus did all this as God's Son, according to God's plan, motivated by God's love. This is how the tension between God's love and his wrath is resolved.

Some people have a problem with this. They call the biblical explanation of the cross immoral. 'How could God punish an innocent third party (Jesus) and so let us off our sins?' they say. They might put it in terms like this: 'If someone had committed a crime, how could it be right to punish his brother or his mother in his place?' Stated like that it seems a fair question. But actually it is to misunderstand something crucial about what the Bible teaches.

One of the most famous references to the cross in the Bible reads like this: 'God demonstrates his own love for us in this: While we were still sinners, Christ died for us.'[u] If we took out the names of God and Christ and replaced them with two ordinary names like Peter and John, you will see something strange happens. It would then read: 'Peter demonstrates his own love for us in this: While we were still sinners, John died for us.' It no longer makes sense. How could the fact that John died for us demonstrate Peter's love for us? The Bible's great statement makes no sense unless God and Christ are essentially one and the same. What God is, Jesus is. Here we begin to touch on the great mysteries of the Trinity, that the one God is three persons — Father, Son and Holy Spirit — and that at the incarnation, God the Son became a human being in Jesus. The Bible is affirming here that Christ, who died at Calvary, is God. At the cross, God the judge was not punishing some innocent third party; rather, he paid for our sin himself. That is the love he has for us. At the cross his anger and mercy meet in the most astonishing way. He, the holy one, took upon himself the just consequences of our sin so that we might be saved.

When God does a work, we know he does it thoroughly. With sins justly and honourably dealt with, we can exchange our sin for righteousness in God's sight through faith in Christ. God clothes us in complete acceptability before his holy presence — and this is because of what he accomplished two thousand years ago on the cross, when Jesus was crucified.

We have thought of the anger of God being revealed, but through the cross of Jesus a righteousness from God is revealed that is offered to all through faith in Jesus Christ. As the Bible puts it: 'I am not ashamed of the gospel [good news], because it is the power of God for the salvation of everyone who believes... For in the gospel a righteousness from God is revealed, a righteousness that is by faith from first to last, just as it is written: "The righteous will live by faith."ᵛ

The present outworking of the judgement of God in society is a slow judgement. In his love God is giving time for the good news of forgiveness and acceptance with himself through faith in Jesus Christ to go out to all. He looks for people to turn to Christ and find forgiveness. There is a sense in which every moment we live is yet another 'second chance' granted to us by God.

Perhaps the greatest untold story of the last century, as far as the secular world is concerned, is that of the spread of the gospel. Though it is never in the headlines of the world's newspapers, nor is it ever spoken of by the secular TV news, this good news of Jesus Christ has been winning the hearts of people in country after country in recent years. Millions have found Christ in China, South America, Africa and the Far East. Judgement is slow, because God is giving the world time.

We should not misuse this window of opportunity. One day it will close. Meanwhile there is a 'day of grace' in which we should seek God by turning from our sins, asking God to clothe us in Christ's righteousness and for Christ to come into our hearts. God earnestly invites us to turn to him and put our faith in Christ.

But finally, there is a third conclusion that the Bible would have us draw from surveying the slow but sure degeneration of our society.

Joyful conversion

If the right and proper wrath of God is being worked out in the gradual unravelling of good, and the hardening of people's hearts to pursue sinful desires, then the mark that someone has truly found God in Christ is that their lives are arrested from the downward slide into degeneracy. They are rescued from the moral and spiritual decline that is going on all around us. If the sign of judgement is that 'God gave them up', then the hallmark of salvation is that, having put our trust in Christ, God so takes hold of our lives that we begin to change for the better, both morally and spiritually. Our conscience is refocused. We find the hand of God upon us, restraining us, guiding and directing us. We find within ourselves a new appetite for God and for goodness.

True conversion to Christ is not a sloppy 'easy-believism' that results in a person simply attending church, but whose life is very little different from the rest of the culture. Do not be fooled. True conversion results in an inward change of heart that leads us away from sin and towards a holy and loving humanity patterned on that of the Lord Jesus Christ. When people become Christians they do not become instantly perfect. Just as it takes a long time to turn around a big ocean-going oil tanker, so it takes time for our lives to turn around. But the point is that our lives really do turn. Jesus said, 'My sheep listen to my voice; I know them, and they follow me. I give them eternal life, and they shall never perish.'w

I have used the word 'joyful', but I could have used 'jubilant' to head this section. In the early part of the Bible, called the Old Testament, the word jubilant is linked to the custom of the year of Jubilee. This occurred every fifty years among God's Old Testament people, Israel. It was the year that all debts were cancelled, all slaves set free and all lost inheritances returned. Obviously it was a time of great joy. But in particular, it was a time when oppression and bondage were revoked. Without Christ, we are enslaved to the decadent ways of our decaying culture. But when we are found by God, as we truly turn to Christ in

faith, then we find ourselves released from that slavery. God gives us a new perspective on life. He gives us new power to change. We acquire a new love for God and a desire to worship and glorify him, which shows itself in the practicalities of the way we live our lives.

Faith in Christ unites us to him and gives us access to new resources. The Bible says, concerning the Lord Jesus Christ, 'The death he died, he died to sin once for all; but the life he lives, he lives to God. In the same way, count yourselves dead to sin but alive to God in Christ Jesus. Therefore do not let sin reign in your mortal body.'[x]

The things of this world no longer have the same attraction. We have found a life and a treasure in Christ, with which nothing else can compare. We enjoy the love of God.

One remarkable Bible passage describes the great change of Christian conversion. Whereas once the person was under God's anger and judgement, it now says that through turning to Christ, they have become 'God's workmanship, created in Christ Jesus to do good works'.[y] The phrase 'God's workmanship' can be legitimately translated 'God's works of art'. Here is an amazing change: from being objects of wrath and judgement, bound for the scrap heap, they become God's masterpieces, which he is still working on to bring to perfection. God invites us all to this joyful transformation of our lives.

An illustration might help to cement into our minds the wonderful opportunity of rescue which is held out before us through turning to Christ. The story is told of a family who lived on the prairies of North America many years ago. It had been a long hot summer and the grass and bushland had become as dry as tinder. One morning the unthinkable happened. The family awoke to see the prairie on fire and the wind blowing the great flames towards their home. The whole horizon was ablaze. They could see they had little chance of survival. They got up, collected a few possessions together and began to run. But the wind was strong and the flames were quickly catching up with them. What on earth could they do? There seemed to be no way out.

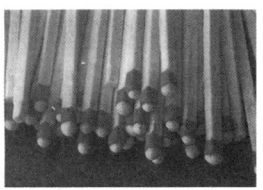

But just then the father, with great insight, had a wonderful idea. He realized that the family could be saved from the fire by fire. He told them all to stop running. He took a box of matches from his pocket and began to light the prairie grass in front of them. 'What are you doing?' the family shouted. It seemed like madness, to create flames in front as well as having them behind them. But the father told them to stand still and watch. The wind continued to blow and, as they remained still, the patch of land before them burned, and the flames raced off ahead. But soon the land immediately in front of them burned out. That patch of ground could no longer provide fuel for a fire. They waited breathlessly as the great prairie fire came leaping up behind them. And as it approached they stepped onto the patch of burned-out land. Here they were safe. Here the prairie fire could not come. Their lives were saved and how they rejoiced.

This gives us one way of understanding the cross of Jesus. There is a great day of judgement coming. It is like that great prairie fire that threatened the family, which must eventually and inevitably catch up with us all. But there is a place where the judgement of God has already fallen. That place is at the cross of Jesus. And it is as if there is a patch of burned-out ground around his cross where sinners like you and I can go and find safety from the coming fire of God. We must be converted. We must turn from our own ways, and submit to God. We must come to Christ and his cross. We must put our faith in Jesus and, openly and unashamedly, take our stand with him.

There is a judgement coming, but refuge and acceptance are found in Jesus Christ, and God is giving us a window of opportunity to be saved through faith in him. The hallmark of that salvation is a release from the darkness of our culture and living for God instead.

These are the conclusions that the Bible would have us take on board as we look out on our unravelling Western world today.

Is God speaking to you? If through what you have read in this booklet you know that God is calling you to Christ, then you should not delay responding to his call. Prayer is simply talking to God on the basis of what Jesus has done for sinners. You should pray, confessing that you, like all of us, are a sinner who has fallen short of the glory of God. You should ask for forgiveness and new life through the finished work of Jesus.

References

1. Frank Furedi, *The Spectator*, January 2002.
2. *The Cost of Family Breakdown*, compiled and edited by David Lindsay, Family Matters, 2000.
3. According to doctors, during the past decade the annual number of new attenders at genito-urinary medicine clinics has escalated to over one million, and cases of gonorrhoea have doubled since 1995. Even greater increases are reported in chlamydial infections, the most common cause of preventable infertility, George Kinghorn, *A sexual health and HIV strategy for England*, British Medical Journal 2001; 323: 243-244.
4. P. Cameron et al, *The Journal of Death and Dying*, 1994, 29, 249-271.
5. Paul writes, 'For everything God created is good, and nothing is to be rejected if it is received with thanksgiving, because it is consecrated by the word of God and prayer,' (1 Timothy 4:4). Later in the same letter he speaks of 'God, who richly provides us with everything for our enjoyment' (1 Timothy 6:17).
6. BBC TV news, February 2002.
7. G. B. Shaw, quoted in *Holding up a mirror: How civilizations decline* by Anne Glyn-Jones, Century, London, 1996, p.443.

Bible references

a. Genesis 2:7
b. Genesis 3:19
c. Romans 1:18
d. Genesis 1:31
e. Romans 1:24, 26-27
f. Romans 1:18
g. Romans 1:28
h. Romans 1:19
i. Romans 1:20
j. Romans 1:24, 26, 28
k. Ephesians 4:18-19
l. Romans 1:25
m. 2 Peter 3:3-10
n. Romans 2:6-10
o. Romans 3:23
p. Romans 1:28
q. 1 Timothy 2:4
r. Exodus 34:6; Numbers 14:18; Psalm 86:15; 145:8
s. Romans 3:21-26
t. Romans 6:23
u. Romans 5:8
v. Romans 1:16-17
w. John 10:27-28
x. Romans 6:10-12
y. Ephesians 2:10

If you need further help, please contact the following: